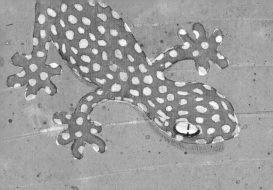

For my grandson, Emerson Bond,
who loves to climb
R. H.

For Mum
B. L.

Text copyright © 2017 by Raymond Huber
Illustrations copyright © 2017 by Brian Lovelock

First U.S. edition 2019

Library of Congress Catalog Card Number pending
ISBN 978-0-7636-9885-0

18 19 20 21 22 23 LEO 10 9 8 7 6 5 4 3 2 1
Printed in Heshan, Guandong, China

This book was typeset in Chapparal Pro, Gararond, and
Journal.
The illustrations were done in watercolor, acrylic ink,
and colored pencil.

Candlewick Press
99 Dover Street
Somerville, Massachusetts 02144

visit us at www.candlewick.com

Gecko

RAYMOND HUBER

illustrated by BRIAN LOVELOCK

CANDLEWICK PRESS

Gecko peeks out of a crack in the cliff.

All clear.

He scurries down the cliff face and stops on a sunbaked ledge to warm up. There are many dangers in the daylight, and Gecko is on high alert.

Geckos are cold-blooded, so they need the sun's heat to keep warm.

They have to be careful when they're out in the open because they have lots of predators. Geckos are eaten by snakes, birds, cats, rats, scorpions, and large spiders.

Gecko cleans himself by licking the grit from his scaly skin. His tongue whisks around his face and wipes his eyes.

The sun will soon set, and Gecko is getting hungry — so hungry, he could eat his own skin!

Most geckos' eyes can't close but are covered by a see-through disk called a spectacle. Geckos' feet are self-cleaning — the rolling movement of their feet sheds dirt as they walk.

Luckily, his outer layer of skin is getting loose; it's the perfect time to peel it. Gecko plucks and picks at his skin and squirms out of it. He peels his eyes, too.

Then Gecko eats the crinkled skin — a snack off his own back.

As geckos grow, they shed an outer layer of dead skin several times a year. Eating the old skin ensures that it won't attract predators.

Gecko beware!

A hawk is hunting. Time to disappear. Gecko's color darkens, and the skin along his sides opens out until he seems to melt into the rock. The hawk wheels away, and Gecko quickly seeks shelter.

Gecko camouflage includes dappled skin patterns and colors, turning lighter or darker, and skin folds that flatten out so that their body casts no shadow.

He jumps onto a tree. What's this creeping toward him? A tasty cockroach! Gecko is as still as a stone until the bug is almost under his nose.

CRUNCH!

He strikes with strong jaws and jerks his head back to swallow the cockroach whole.

Geckos eat insects, worms, fruit, and sometimes other smaller lizards. They have between fifty and three hundred tiny teeth.

It's dark now and Gecko climbs
higher to search for flying food.
He weaves between leaves, slinks
along branches, and trickles over twigs,
his tongue flicking out to smell the air.
Gecko dangles from a branch and
snatches a mosquito, the first of
many that night.

Most geckos are active at night.
Their big eyes help them see in the
dark. Geckos smell with their
noses and tongues.

In the morning, Gecko finds a shady overhang where he can snooze for the day. He clings upside down on the smooth rock. But Gecko doesn't see the rat watching from the shadows.

Geckos' feet have a powerful grip because of millions of hairlike structures called setae on their toe pads. Each tiny seta has hundreds of tips, which enable a gecko to hold on to any surface.

The rat shoots out!

Gecko hears the clip of claws just in time. He kicks off the rock and nosedives onto a ledge below.

Go, Gecko, go!

Geckos have excellent hearing. They are fast runners and nimble movers, with a flexible backbone and a tail that helps them balance.

The rat leaps!

The rat lands on Gecko's tail, pinning him down. Gecko drops his tail, runs into a crevice, and wedges himself in. Will his tail trick fool the rat?

A gecko can break off all or part of its tail. The disconnected tail still squirms, distracting or deceiving a predator while the gecko escapes.

Gecko waits a while, then pokes his head up. The rat is gone, but what's this? Gecko's dropped tail has only been partially eaten. Gecko carries it back into the cranny and devours it himself.

If a predator doesn't eat a dropped gecko tail, the gecko will. It's full of fat, too good to waste. A new tail will grow within four months.

As night falls once more, Gecko skitters to the top of the cliff. His sharp eyes spy a flash of color below — the freckled skin of another gecko. He must warn this intruder off his territory.

Geckos are one of the few animals in the world that can see colors at night.

Most male geckos won't allow other males in their area.

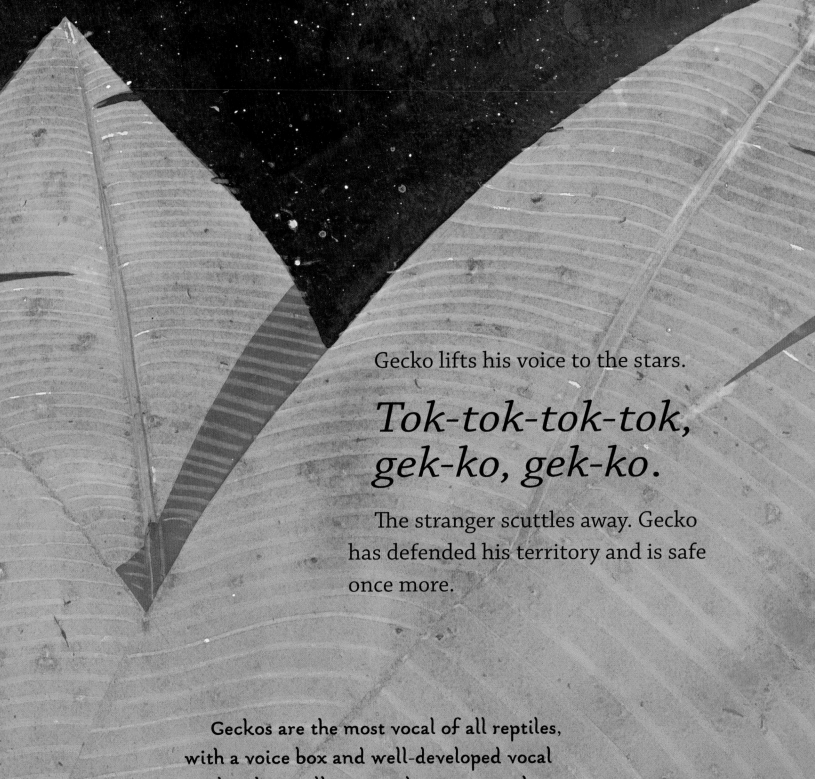

Gecko lifts his voice to the stars.

Tok-tok-tok-tok, gek-ko, gek-ko.

The stranger scuttles away. Gecko has defended his territory and is safe once more.

Geckos are the most vocal of all reptiles, with a voice box and well-developed vocal cords. Their calls are used to scare rivals and predators, to signal danger, or to attract a mate. The name *gecko* probably comes from the sounds they make.

MORE ABOUT GECKOS

Geckos are the escape artists of the lizard world, able to outsmart predators with disguises, deceptions, and fast getaways. Geckos can live on rocky mountains or tropical islands, in hot deserts or rain forests, and even in cities. More than 1,500 different kinds of geckos have made their homes on every continent except Antarctica. Geckos are one of the most important creatures for controlling insects such as mosquitoes and flies, and many species help pollinate plants. The gecko in this book is a tokay.

INDEX

Look up the pages to find out all about gecko things.
Don't forget to look at both kinds of words —
this kind and **this kind**.

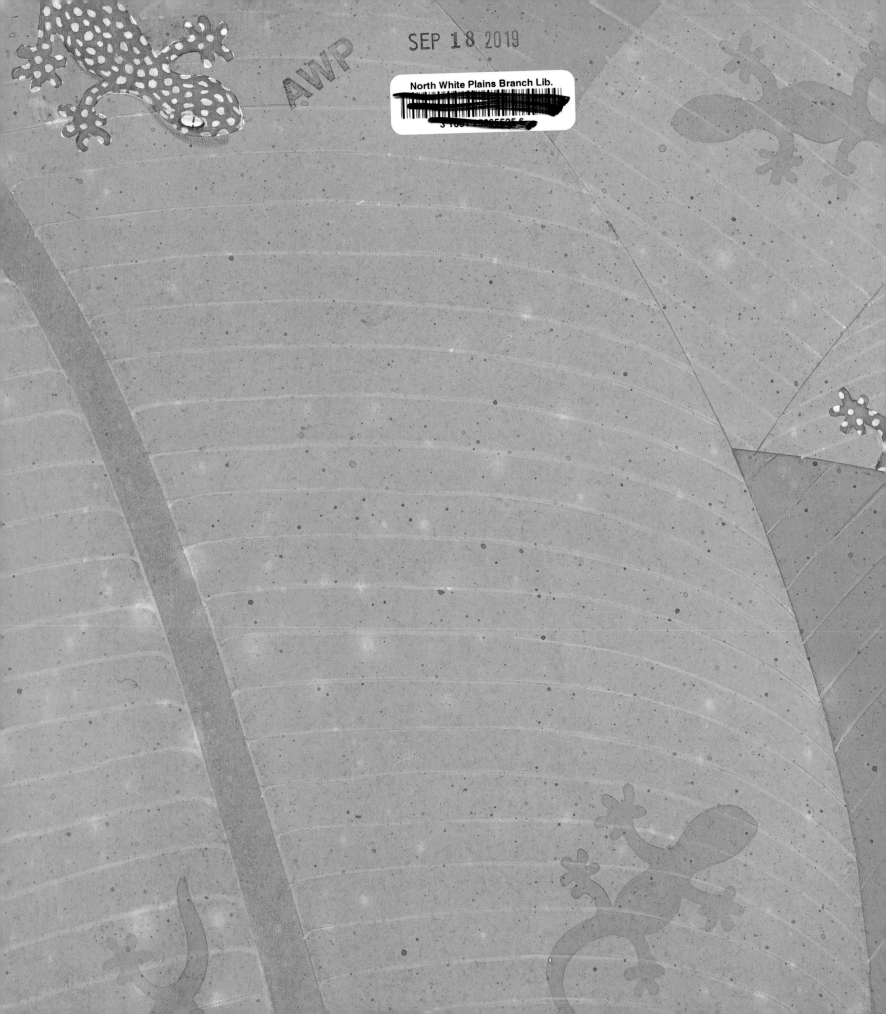